The Great Napoleon for Children

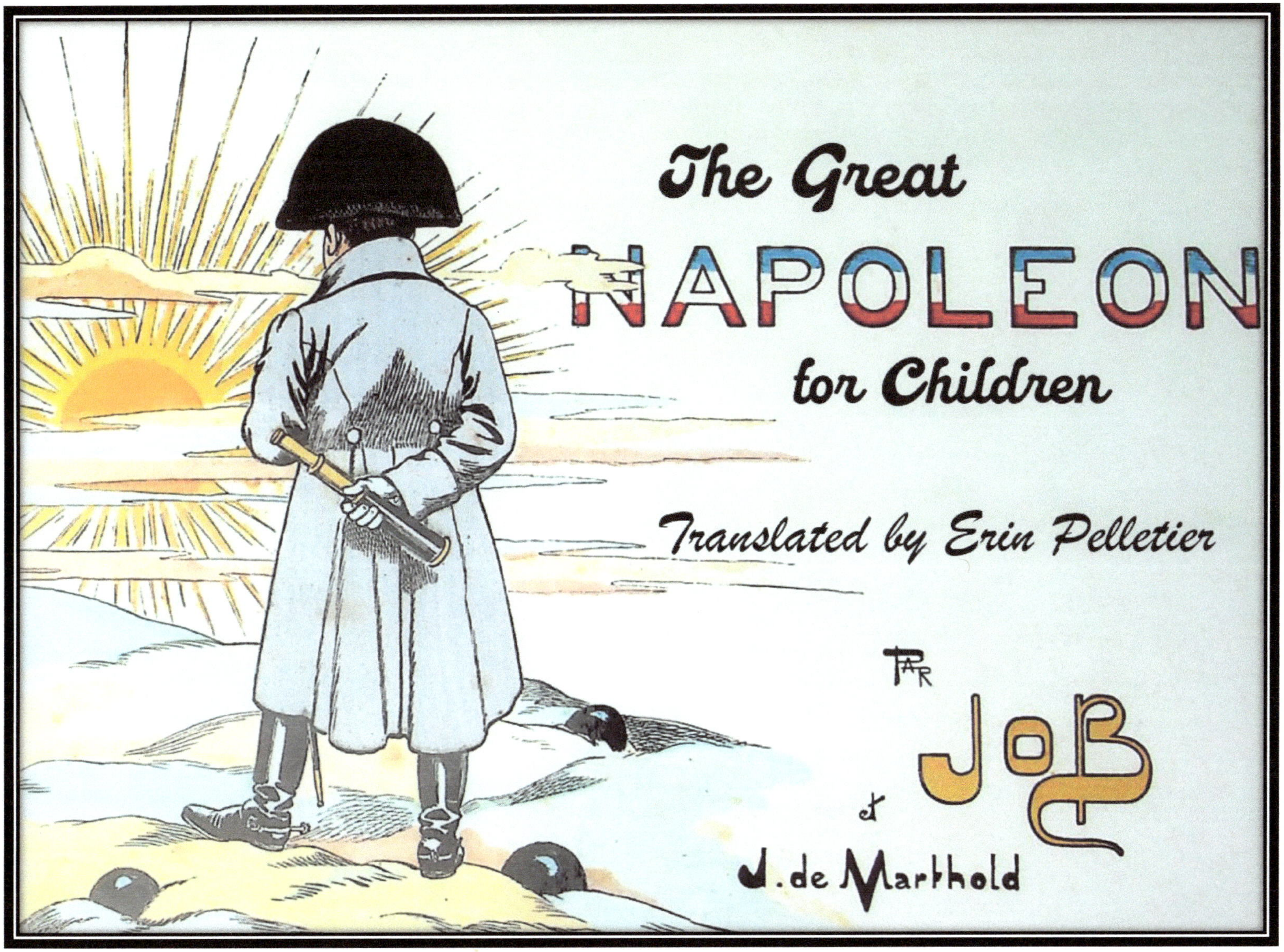

The Great NAPOLEON for Children

Translated by Erin Pelletier

Par JOB et J. de Marthold

LITTLE FROG HILL
ANTELOPE HILL PUBLISHING

Translation Copyright © 2024 Antelope Hill Publishing

The Great Napoleon for Children is a translation from French of
Le Grand Napoléon des Petits Enfants originally published by Éditions Plon, Paris, 1893.
First Antelope Hill edition, first printing 2024.

Written and illustrated by J. de Marthold.

Translated by Erin Pelletier, 2024.

Layout by Sebastian Durant.

Published by Little Frog Hill, the children's imprint of
Antelope Hill Publishing | antelopehillpublishing.com

Hardcover ISBN-13: 979-8-89252-024-9

Once upon a time, there was a pristine isle called Corsica.

August 15th, 1769

A child was born there in Ajaccio, in a room draped with tapestries depicting Homeric heroes.

1779

His father brought him to Versailles, where he saw for the first time a king, Louis XVI, whom he would succeed.

1785

As a lieutenant in Valence, he rises at dawn,

supervises the fire drills,

and those of the artillery,

and each day he makes night rounds.

1786

While he was garrisoned in Valence, he took advantage of the opportunity to study the *Digeste* and to strengthen his knowledge of law.

June 20th, 1792

He sees Louis XVI for the second time.
"Swap the crown for a revolutionary's red bonnet!" he said.
And he thought, "Trade the cap for a crown . . . ?"

September 12th-December 20th, 1793

At the siege of Toulin, he loaded a cannon like an ordinary soldier.
He was injured and his wound became infected.

1795

A famine in Paris caused a strong fisherwoman to reproach him for fattening himself up at the expense of the people. "Madam," he replied with a smile, "take a good look at me and tell me which of us is fatter?"

February 23rd, 1796

He was appointed General-in-Chief of the Army of Italy.

He promised the soldiers victories. And he kept his promise.

March 9th, 1796

Master Raguideau, the notary of the widow Beauharnais,
spoke to her unaware that he was being overheard.
He said, "You! Marry that little Bonaparte, a soldier with nothing but a cloak and a sword?!"

May 10th, 1796

After the Battle of Lodi, the veterans offered their young leader the rank of corporal. This was the origin of the nickname *Petit Caporal* (Little Corporal), which has remained with him to this day.

July 1st, 1798

Napoleon landed in the land of the Pharaohs, and he explored everywhere.
He was followed by a commission of scholars and
artists who had never ridden on the backs of camels before.

1798

Napoleon tested the Sphinx and thought that he
heard the monster whisper the word, "Immortality!"

July 24th, 1798

He said, "Soldiers! From the summit of these pyramids, forty centuries look down upon you!" And the victory was achieved.

May 16th, 1800

He crossed the Great Saint Bernard Pass on a mule,
guided by a young man whom he rewarded generously.

June 14th, 1800

"Three hours!" cried General Desaix. "The battle is lost!"
"Three hours!" Napoleon said calmly. "We still have time to win!"
It was the Battle of Marengo.

December 24th, 1800

On Rue Saint-Nicaise, he miraculously escaped the explosion of an infernal machine.

November 9th, 1801

He celebrated the year of peace with a magnificent festival.

May 19th, 1802

Napoleon founded the Order of the Legion of Honor. Immediately, Parisians were seen imitating the ribbon of the order by wearing red carnations.

September 2nd-20th, 1803

At his camp in Boulogne, he ceaselessly turned his eyes toward England.

December 2nd, 1804

On the morning of his coronation, Napoleon saw Joséphine's notary.
He said to him with a laugh:
"Well, Master Raguideau, here's the cape! And here's the sword!"

October 1st, 1805

He crosses the Rhine at Kehl . . .

. . . and obtains the allegiance of the Elector of Baden.

December 1st, 1805

He fell asleep, peacefully, on a dark night.
He was awakened by the first rays of the Austerlitz sun.

1805

The Old Guard trained their dogs to salute the emperor. And he returned the salute.

October 27th, 1806

Followed by the French army . . .

. . . he entered Berlin.

February 8th, 1807

At the Battle of Eylau, the bloodiest of his victories, people were killed next to gravestones.

May 24th, 1807

After victory at the Siege of Danzig, he said to Lefebvre, "Do you like chocolate?"
Lefebvre answered, "Not at all, Sire, I loathe it."
"You should take this one," Napoleon replied.
Surprised and charmed by what he saw in the packet, Lefebvre exclaimed, "Sire! The best chocolate is a chocolate that comes with a hundred thousand livres and the title of duke!"

July 7th, 1807

After signing the Treaties of Tilsit, he inspected the French army.

The soldiers of foreign leaders saluted Napoleon and his guard.

May 22nd, 1809

At the Battle of Essling, while he hastily ate a simple meal,
he was told of the death of Lannes, his best friend.

May 22nd, 1809

On the island of Lobau, Napoleon followed the events of the battle from the top of a fir tree.

May 27th, 1810

Napoleon went to meet Marie-Louise, Archduchess of Austria, whom he was to marry.

1811

Master of the world, and now the happiest of fathers. Napoleon watches as his son, the king of Rome, takes his first ride in his goat carriage.

September 15th-16th, 1812

In Moscow, the flames endanger his victory.

As he crossed the Berezina River, the cold tears it away.

October 18th, 1813

"Pardon, apologies, Sire!"

February 10th-11th, 1814

On the evening of the Battle of Champaubert, which was the day before the Battle of Montmirail, a pensive Napoleon holds the child of a canteen maid.

March 16th, 1814

After the Battle of Reims, he watched the last contingent of the French campaign march past. He exclaimed, "Come on, Bonaparte, save Napoleon!"

March 7th, 1815

On his return from Elba, the gates of Grenoble were dismantled for him.
"The fatherland is reopening before me," he said.

June 18th, 1815

He fell for the first time, defeated, in a place that geography calls Waterloo—a place that history calls Treason. On this day, Cambronne said his last word.

July 15th, 1815

He embarked on the *Bellérophon*. . . .
Alive, he would never set foot on French soil again.

October 15th, 1815

He was confined to St. Helena. At night, this rock looks like a little hat.
Only one light shines on St. Helena—the light of Napoleon's
genius as he dictates his memoir, the *Mémorial*.

May 5th, 1821

He ascended into glory, and his eagle died.

Everything passes, except memory

In memory of the Little Corporal, a cabaret owner named his restaurant "The Tomb of the Great Man."

The name was banned as seditious, so he substituted it with this unsubtle translation, "The Beer of Mars."

ENJOYED THIS BOOK?

TO READ MORE, VISIT US AT

ANTELOPEHILLPUBLISHING.COM

www.ingramcontent.com/pod-product-compliance
Lightning Source LLC
Chambersburg PA
CBHW050847010526
44107CB00017BA/1207